W9-ATB-400

For my nieces Ava & Lyric,
You two will always be my little sprouts.

ABC's
for
Little Sprouts

By Cate Chauntee

Copyright © 2021 by Caitlyne Gonzalez

All rights reserved. No part of this book may be reproduced in any form on by an electronic or mechanical means, including information storage and retrieval systems, without permission in writing from the publisher, except by a reviewer who may quote brief passages in a review.

First printing edition in 2021 in United States

Book design by Caitlyne Gonzalez
Written by Caitlyne Gonzalez
Illustrations by Olga Rizhkova

ISBN-978-0-578-30668-1
Published by Cate Chauntee

For information, contact **cate.chauntee@gmail.com**

A

is for...

Did you know aloe is used to help treat boo-boos like scrapes and cuts?

Aloe

B

is for...

Bamboo is one of the fastest growing plants on the planet!

Bamboo

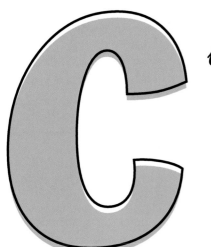 **C** *is for...*

 Did you know a cactus can survive in snowy climates too?

Cactus

D is for...

Meaning "Female Dragon", this plant is related to asparagus!

Dracaena
[druh-SEE-nuh]

E is for...

Eucalyptus is one of the TALLEST plants, reaching up to 200 feet!

Eucalyptus

F is for...

BEWARE!
This plant is toxic to dogs, cats, horses, even children!

Fiddle Leaf

G is for...

Don't move this ficus around too much or it will drop it's leaves!

Gingseng Ficus

H

is for...

Some of these plants are edible and found in Japanese cuisines

Hosta

I is for...

Birds enjoy using this plant for shade, shelter, and to hibernate and nest

Ivy Tree

J is for...

Did you know this plant is a yummy snack for tortoises?

Jade Plant

K is for...

This is one slow grower... taking about five years to fully grow

Kentia Palm

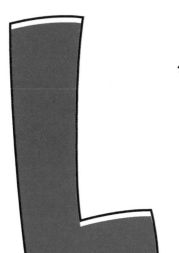 is for...

 Pucker Up! This plant has flower buds that peek out of dark tubes, that look like small lipsticks

Lipstick Plant

M is for...

This plant is nicknamed the "Swiss Cheese Plant" because of the many holes in their leaves

Monstera

N is for...

This is a Prayer Plant, meaning that it's leaves close upward at night

Never-Never Plant

O is for...

There are over 25,000 species of Orchids! The smallest is the size of a dime

Orchid

P is for...

Peace Lilies are great house plants because they help keep the air clean

Peace Lily

Q

is for...

Unlike other plants, Quinoa is a "Superfood" with lots of protein!

Quinoa

R is for...

This is also a Prayer Plant, their leaves close at night and reopen in the morning

Rattlesnake Plant

S is for...

Unlike most plants, this one gives off oxygen at NIGHT so you can sleep well

Snake Plant

T

is for...

Taro is used as a vegetable and can be eaten but ONLY if it's cooked!

Taro

U is for...

This plant grows over 49 feet and has leaflets that look like umbrellas

Umbrella Plant

V is for...

Violets have heart-shaped leaves and are used in many perfumes

Violet

W is for...

The shape of this palm's leaves give it a windmill appearance and is covered with brown hairy fibers

Windmill Palm

X *is for...*

Also known as "Bear Grass", this plant can survive harsh FIRES!

Xerophyllum
[zee-ro-FILL-um]

Y is for...

Did you know Yucca can survive up to 1,000 years in the wild?

Yucca

Z is for...

Nicknamed the "Unkillable Plant", it can survive for months without water

ZZ Plant

The End!

Now you know your ABC's,
Next time won't you plant with me?

Thank you, Reader!

I really hope you enjoyed learning the Alphabet with **ABC's For Little Sprouts.** I myself have loved learning about new plants and have five of my own so far!

If you loved this ABC book and think other little sprouts will too, please leave a review to let us know!
- Cate Chauntee

To learn more about Cate's favorite plants and other publications coming up in the future, follow her on Amazon or Instagram **@Cate.Chauntee**

Made in the USA
Middletown, DE
02 December 2021

53994210R00020